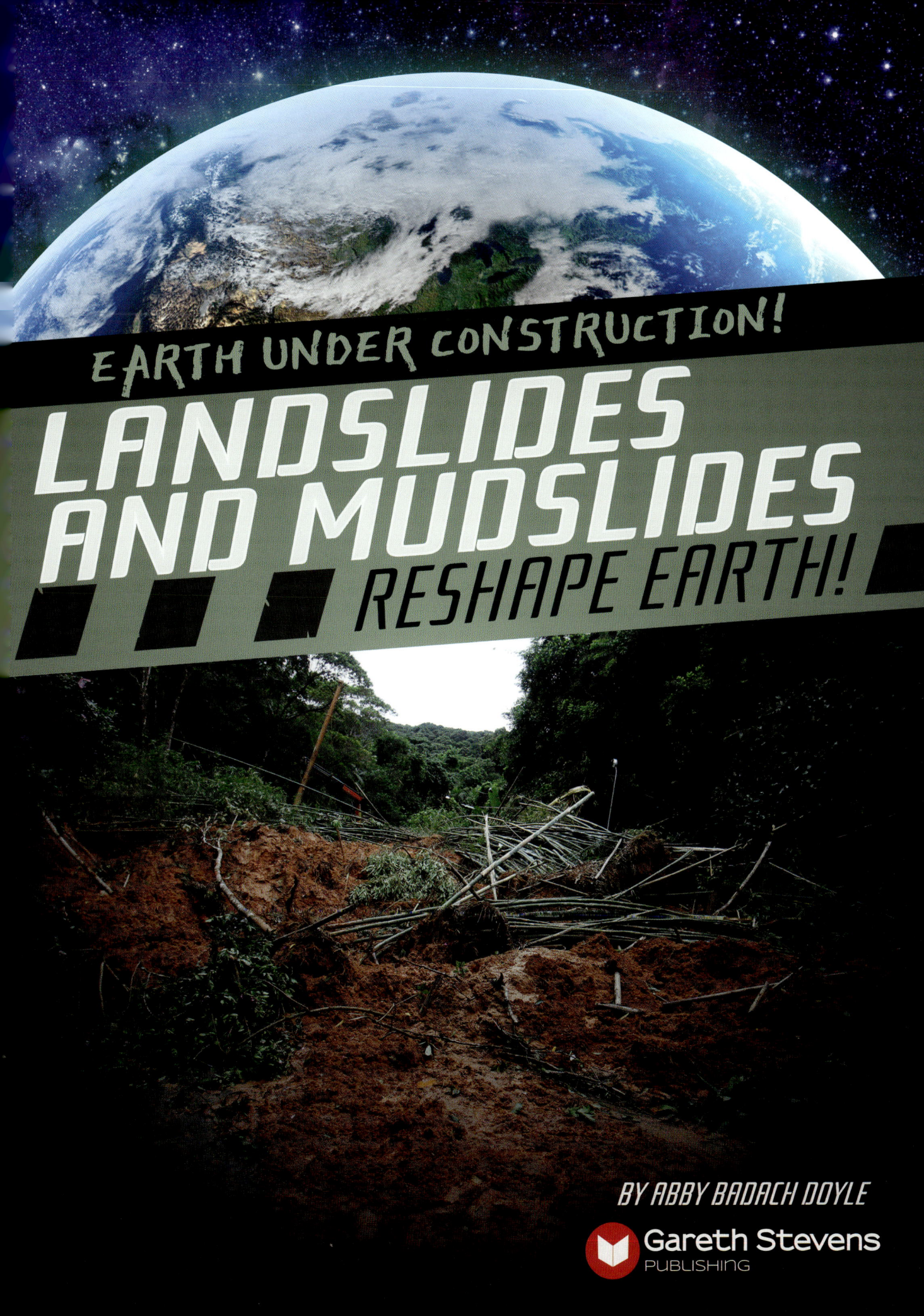

Earth Under Construction!
LANDSLIDES AND MUDSLIDES RESHAPE EARTH!

BY ABBY BADACH DOYLE

Gareth Stevens
PUBLISHING

Please visit our website, www.garethstevens.com. For a free color catalog of all our high-quality books, call toll free 1-800-542-2595 or fax 1-877-542-2596.

Cataloging-in-Publication Data

Names: Doyle, Abby Badach.
Title: Landslides and mudslides reshape Earth! / Abby Badach Doyle.
Description: New York : Gareth Stevens Publishing, 2021. | Series: Earth under construction! | Includes glossary and index.
Identifiers: ISBN 9781538258309 (pbk.) | ISBN 9781538258323 (library bound) | ISBN 9781538258316 (6 pack)
Subjects: LCSH: Landslides–Juvenile literature. | Mudslides–Juvenile literature.
Classification: LCC QE599.A2 D69 2021 | DDC 551.307–dc23

First Edition

Published in 2021 by
Gareth Stevens Publishing
111 East 14th Street, Suite 349
New York, NY 10003

Copyright © 2021 Gareth Stevens Publishing

Designer: Sarah Liddell
Editor: Kate Mikoley

Photo credits: Cover, p. 1 N. Antoine/Shutterstock.com; space background and Earth image used throughout Aphelleon/Shutterstock.com; caution tape used throughout Red sun design/Shutterstock.com; p. 5 JIJI PRESS/Stringer/AFP/Getty Images; p. 7 Cavan Images/Cavan/Getty Images; p. 9 Amit kg/Shutterstock.com; p. 11 zombiu26/Shutterstock.com; p. 13 Michael Duff/Moment/Getty Images; p. 15 PSboom/Shutterstock.com; p. 17 ORLANDO SIERRA/Staff/AFP/Getty Images; p. 19 John T. Barr/Contributor/Hulton Archive/Getty Images; p. 21 Smith Collection/Gado/Contributor/Getty Images; p. 23 Mario Tama/Staff/Getty Images News/Getty Images; p. 25 AFP Contributor/Contributor/DPA/Getty Images; p. 27 (all) photos courtesy of NASA; p. 29 Andrea Toffaletti/500px/500px/Getty Images.

All rights reserved. No part of this book may be reproduced in any form without permission in writing from the publisher, except by a reviewer.

Printed in the United States of America

Some of the images in this book illustrate individuals who are models. The depictions do not imply actual situations or events.

CPSIA compliance information: Batch #CS20GS: For further information contact Gareth Stevens, New York, New York at 1-800-542-2595.

Find us on

CONTENTS

Look Out! 4
What's the Difference? 6
How They Form 8
Types of Landslides 10
Where They Strike 14
How Bad Can They Be? 16
Mount Saint Helens 18
Earthquakes and Landslides 20
Hurricanes and Landslides 22
Can We Prevent Them? 24
Our Changing Planet 28
Glossary 30
For More Information 31
Index 32

Words in the glossary appear in **bold** type the first time they are used in the text.

LOOK OUT!

Landslides and mudslides are some of the most dangerous forces in nature. These roaring rivers of earth and rocks can uproot trees, flip cars, and destroy whole neighborhoods. Sometimes they happen slowly. Other times, they happen in seconds with no warning at all.

Believe it or not, the fastest mudslides can travel at speeds up to 50 miles (80.5 km) per hour! Geologists, or scientists who study the physical forms of Earth, work hard to understand how they happen. The more we learn about these events, the more we can do to protect the people and places that get in their way.

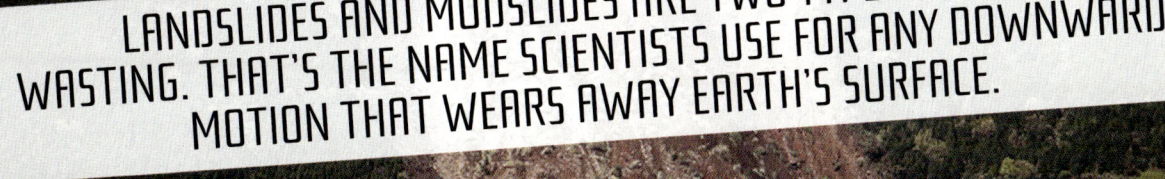

LANDSLIDES AND MUDSLIDES ARE TWO TYPES OF MASS WASTING. THAT'S THE NAME SCIENTISTS USE FOR ANY DOWNWARD MOTION THAT WEARS AWAY EARTH'S SURFACE.

CLEANUP IS EXPENSIVE

Landslides have happened in all 50 states. Every year, they cause billions of dollars in **damage**. That includes private costs, like the price of materials, or matter to build things, and labor to fix someone's ruined house. It also includes public costs to repair things we all use, like roads and electric lines.

WHAT'S THE DIFFERENCE?

Most types of mass wasting start the same way. A big event, like heavy rain or an **earthquake**, loosens the earth. Then, gravity pulls it down or away. Geologists have different names for these events, depending on where they happen and what's in them.

A landslide is any movement of rock or earth that travels down a slope. A landslide is more solid than a mudslide. A mudslide has more water, moves faster, and flows like a liquid. Even though they are different, many people use the word "landslide" as a general term to mean any type of mass wasting down a slope.

A LANDSLIDE CAN ALSO CARRY **DEBRIS**, SUCH AS UPROOTED TREES OR PLANTS.

OTHER NAMES TO KNOW

If a landslide has mostly big rocks that roll downhill, it's called a rockfall or rockslide. An avalanche is a type of landslide with snow and ice. If a landslide happens on the slope of a **volcano**, it's known as a lahar (luh-HAR). The word lahar comes from Indonesia.

HOW THEY FORM

Three main **factors** contribute to landslides: geology, morphology (mor-FAW-luh-gee), and human activity. Geology **refers** to what makes up the rocks or soil. Is it strong and solid, or does it break apart easily? Certain types of rock, such as limestone and sandstone, are more likely to **erode** and cause a slide.

Morphology describes how the land is affected by what is on or around it. For example, ocean waves might wear away a cliff, or a wildfire might burn vegetation that holds soil in place. Finally, human activity like construction, farming, and mining can change the shape of Earth and lead to landslides.

BUILDING A ROAD CAN CHANGE THE WAY WATER DRAINS IN AN AREA. IT CAN ALSO ALTER THE SLOPE OF A NEARBY HILL. BOTH OF THESE THINGS CAN LEAD TO LANDSLIDES.

WATCH OUT FOR WATER

Water is another contributing factor to landslides, especially mudslides. It can show up as rain, melting snow, increased groundwater, or changes in lakes or rivers. Water makes soil and rocks slippery and move more easily. That's why mudflows and debris flows often happen at the same time as a flood.

TYPES OF LANDSLIDES

Scientists put landslides in categories based on how the earth moves when it comes loose. There are many smaller categories. The five biggest are falls, topples, slides, flows, and lateral spreads. Each type can occur with rocks, soil, or both.

Falls and topples are similar. In both cases, rock breaks off and falls down a slope or cliff. Rocks go straight down in a fall. In a topple, they rotate. A slide occurs when a top layer of earth comes loose and slides all at once on a layer underneath. For example, an earthquake might shake soil loose to slide on slippery shale bedrock.

FIVE TYPES OF LANDSLIDES

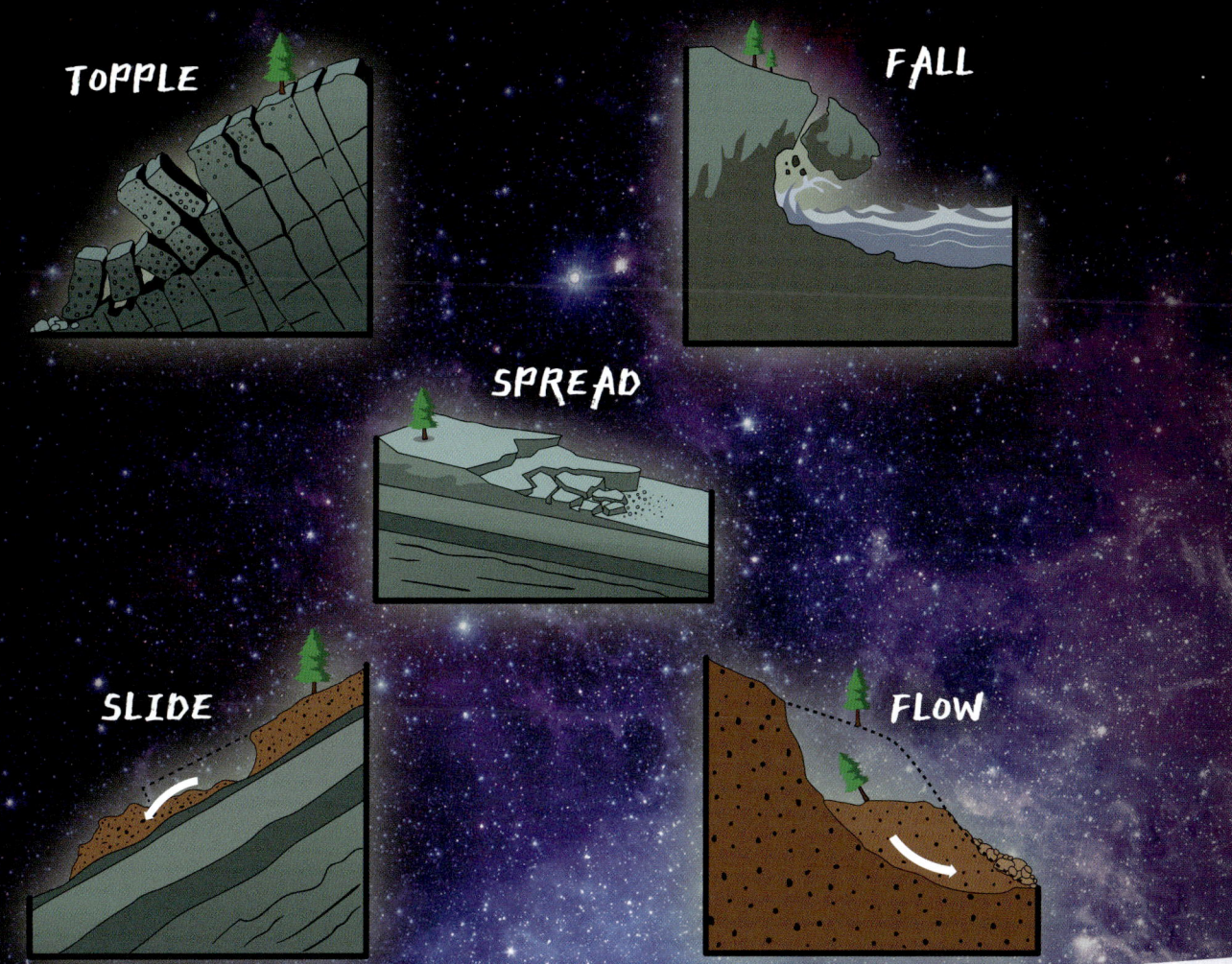

LANDSLIDE IS THE GENERAL TERM, BUT EARTH CAN MOVE IN MORE WAYS THAN JUST SLIDING. IF TWO OR MORE OF THESE MOVEMENTS HAPPEN TOGETHER, IT IS KNOWN AS A **COMPLEX** LANDSLIDE.

ROCKFALLS IN YOSEMITE

In recent years, Yosemite National Park in California, with its many steep cliffs, has had many rockfalls each year. More than 1,000 rockfalls have been recorded there in the past 150 years. This can be dangerous for hikers and rock climbers. Trail crews work hard to keep visitors safe and clear the trails of debris.

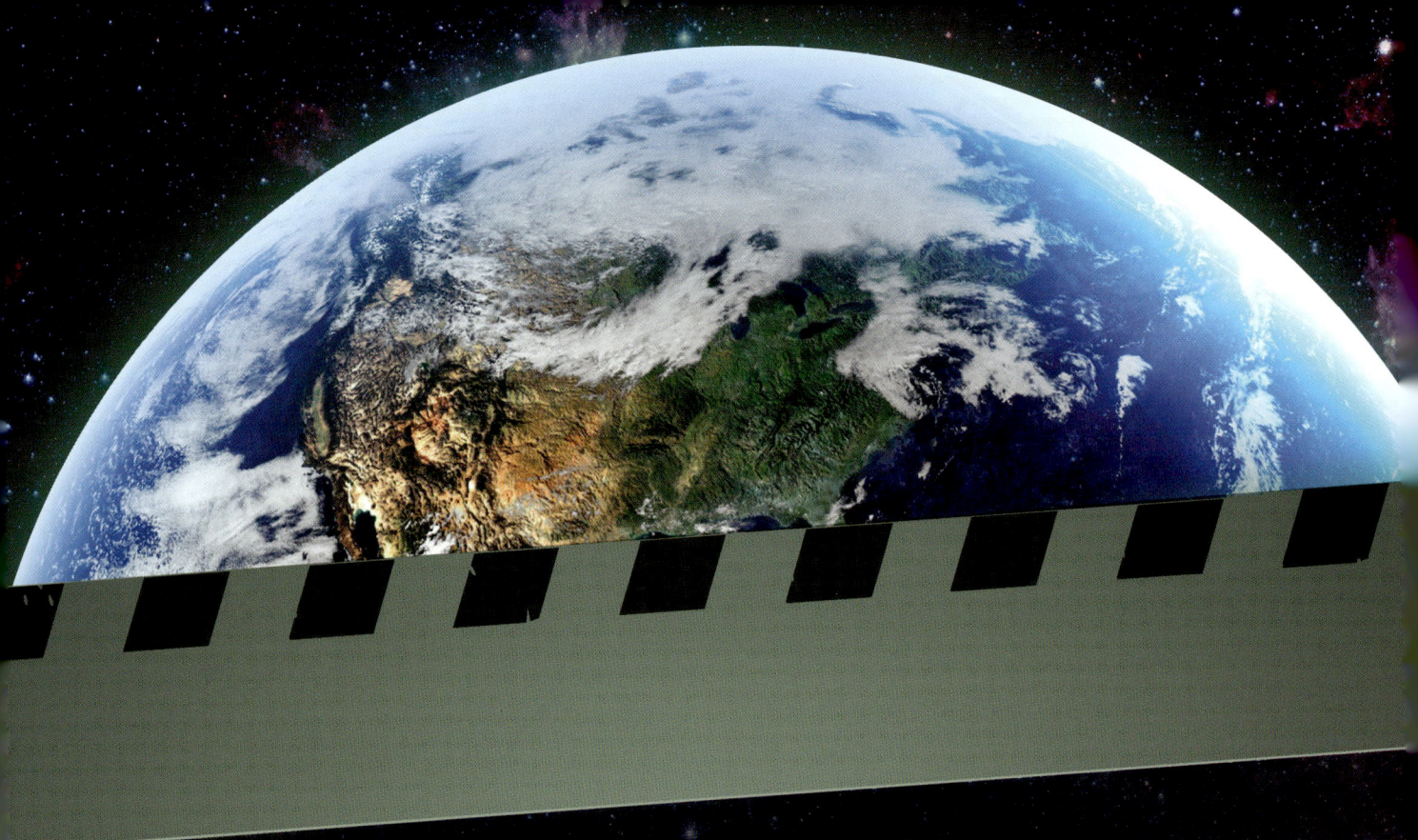

The next category of landslide is called a flow. In most cases, flows make the ground move downhill very fast. A flow can be mostly dry rocks, called a debris flow. Or it might be a thick, wet mix of dust and water, called a mudflow. A mudflow looks a bit like melted chocolate or soft-serve ice cream.

Lastly, a spread is a type of landslide that occurs on slopes so gentle they are almost flat. This happens during earthquakes. In a spread, the earth moves sideways and the top layer of loose soil, often sand or silt, spreads out like a liquid.

IN A MUDFLOW, MOST OF THE SOLIDS ARE SMALLER THAN A GRAIN OF SAND. IN A DEBRIS FLOW, MOST OF THE SOLIDS ARE SAND-SIZED OR LARGER.

SLOW AND STEADY

One type of flow, called creep, moves very slowly. It can go on for years, or even centuries! Creep sometimes happens when soil freezes and thaws, or melts, over time. It happens too slowly to see it, but you can spot its effects such as ripples in the soil or tilted fences or tree trunks.

WHERE THEY STRIKE

Landslides occur in all 50 U.S. states and on all seven continents. At a basic level, a landslide needs a slope in order to form. The slope can be huge, like a mountain or volcano. It can also be small, like a hill that's blocked by a wall along a highway.

Landslides are more likely to happen in places where they have occurred in the past. Areas with heavy rain, earthquakes, or forest fires see landslides more often too. In the United States, the worst landslides happen in mountainous areas like the Appalachians, Rockies, and Pacific Coast.

LANDSLIDE OVERVIEW MAP OF THE U.S.

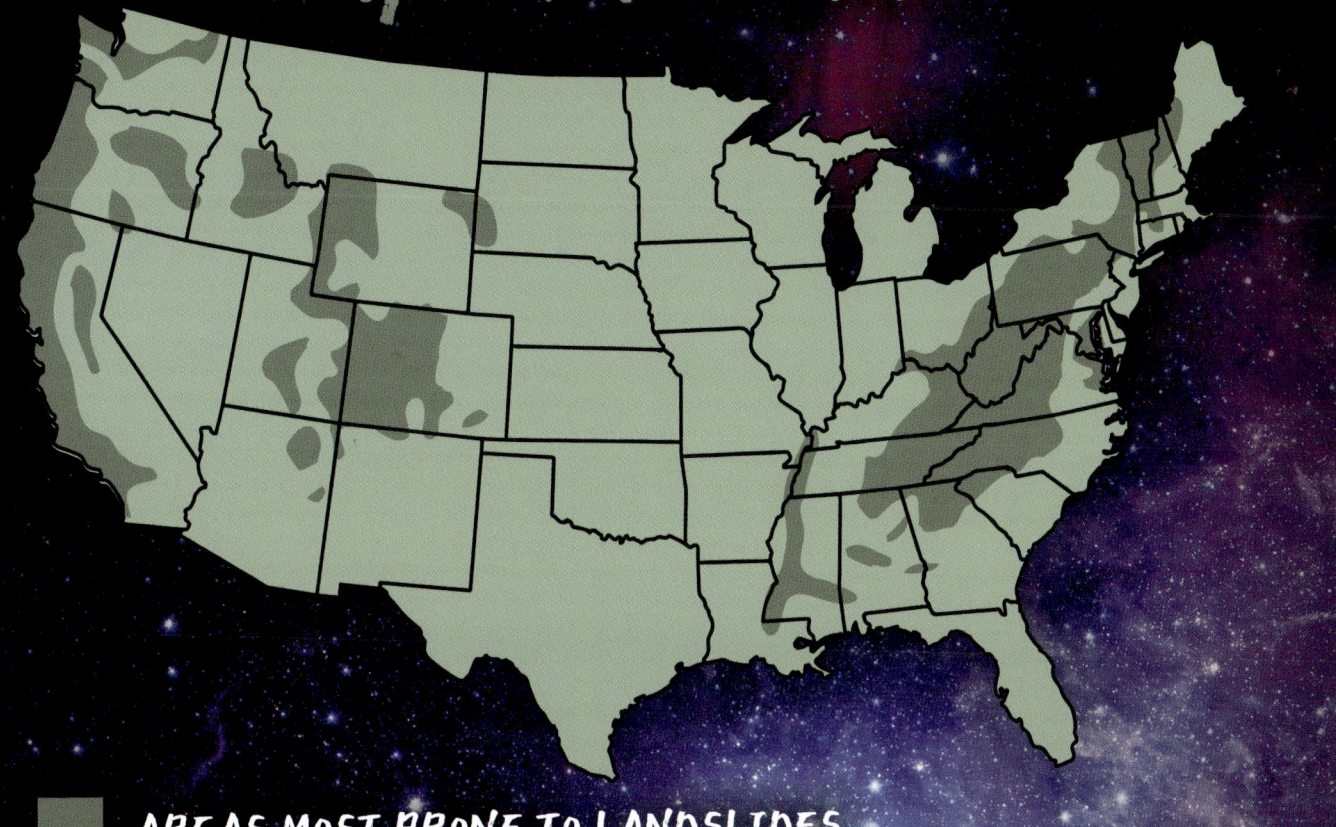

■ AREAS MOST PRONE TO LANDSLIDES

THE U.S. GEOLOGICAL SURVEY, OR USGS, IS THE GOVERNMENT GROUP THAT TRACKS LANDSLIDES. THIS MAP SHOWS THE GENERAL AREAS IN THE U.S. THAT ARE MOST PRONE TO LANDSLIDES.

AROUND THE WORLD

Other countries with frequent landslides include Italy, Austria, China, the Philippines, and Ethiopia. South America has experienced serious landslides too. Many times, harm caused by a landslide is worse in poor countries. These places might lack resources, such as early warning systems or **transportation** that could help prevent deaths.

HOW BAD CAN THEY BE?

If you know a landslide is coming, get out of the way—fast! Debris can destroy or hurt everything in its path, including people and animals. A slide can also block roads and railways that can help people escape or get medical care. Landslides can also break electric, gas, water, and sewage lines. That can cause more people to get hurt and cause the spread of illnesses.

According to the USGS, the deadliest landslide types are rockfalls, debris flows, and lahars. In the United States, as many as 50 people are killed by landslides and debris flows every year. Around the world, deaths from landslides number in the thousands each year.

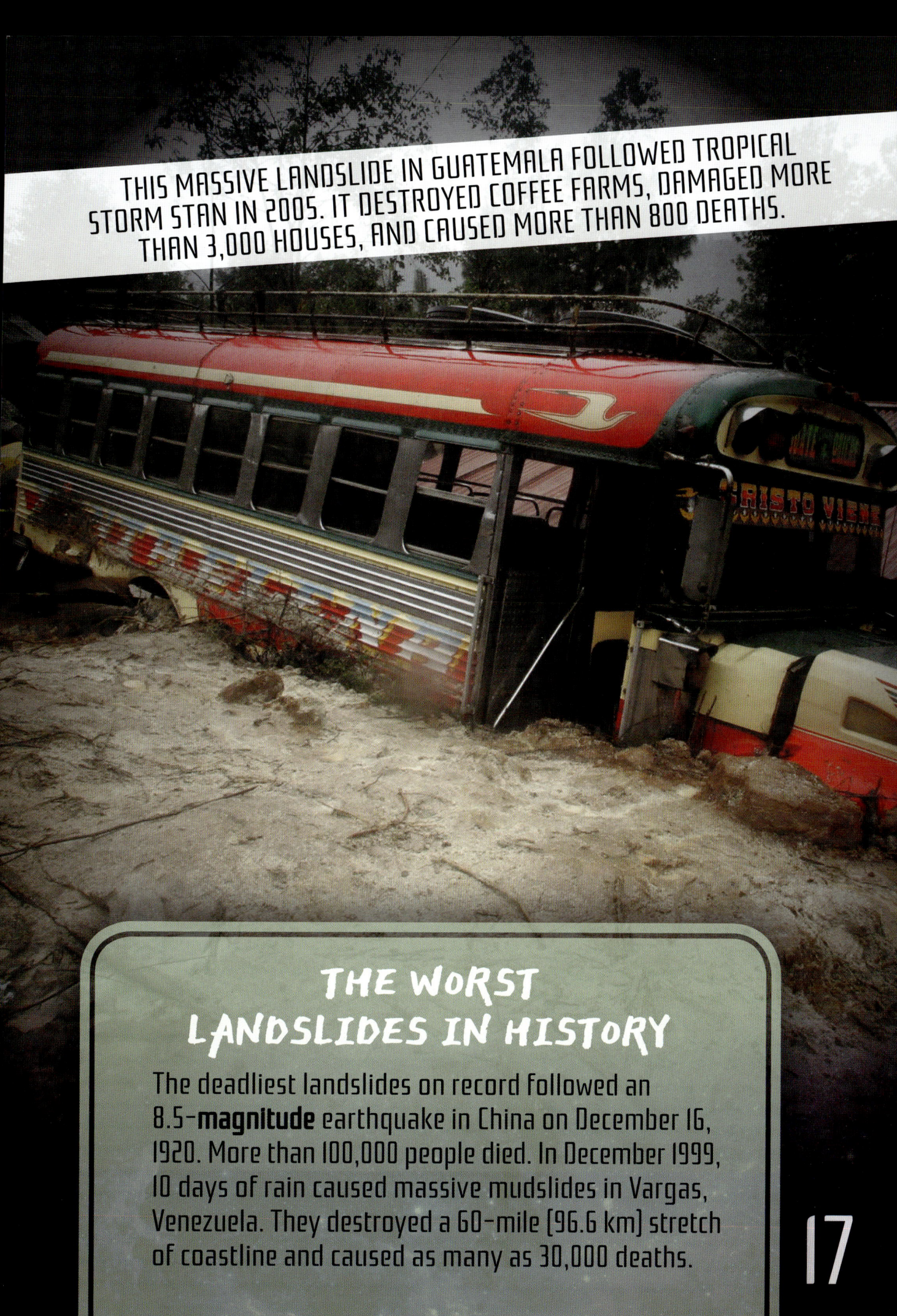

THIS MASSIVE LANDSLIDE IN GUATEMALA FOLLOWED TROPICAL STORM STAN IN 2005. IT DESTROYED COFFEE FARMS, DAMAGED MORE THAN 3,000 HOUSES, AND CAUSED MORE THAN 800 DEATHS.

THE WORST LANDSLIDES IN HISTORY

The deadliest landslides on record followed an 8.5-**magnitude** earthquake in China on December 16, 1920. More than 100,000 people died. In December 1999, 10 days of rain caused massive mudslides in Vargas, Venezuela. They destroyed a 60-mile (96.6 km) stretch of coastline and caused as many as 30,000 deaths.

17

MOUNT SAINT HELENS

Mount Saint Helens, a volcano in Washington state, famously erupted on May 18, 1980. An earthquake caused the eruption and the landslide that followed. The powerful blast knocked 1,312 feet (400 m) of rock and soil from the mountain's peak. Witnesses saw huge trees break like toothpicks from the blast. Then, that debris from the mountaintop tumbled into the North Fork Toutle River.

The river flooded and carried the debris for 14 miles (22.5 km). It destroyed nearly everything in its path. More than 50 people died. By volume, this was one of the largest landslides in recorded history. The debris could have filled 250 million dump trucks!

THE MOUNT SAINT HELENS LANDSLIDE IS SHOWN HERE. ITS DEEPEST POINT MEASURED 600 FEET (182.9 M) DEEP. THAT'S ABOUT AS TALL AS TWO STATUES OF LIBERTY STACKED ON TOP OF EACH OTHER.

VOLCANOES AND LANDSLIDES

Why are landslides common on volcanoes? For starters, volcanoes are usually tall and steep. Compared to other mountains, they are weaker or more unstable. Volcanoes often have layers of loose debris and hot, liquid rock below. An event like an earthquake, eruption, or even heavy rain can **trigger** a landslide in these conditions.

EARTHQUAKES AND LANDSLIDES

Friction is the force that causes things to stick together when they touch. Friction is what makes tiny pieces of dirt cling to each other and the bedrock below, even on an incline. When the ground moves, it breaks up the force of friction. This causes gravity to become stronger than friction. That's why it's common for landslides to follow earthquakes.

Earthquakes also make it easier for water to slip into the openings created from the moving earth. This makes the ground even weaker and more slippery. One of the worst landslides from an earthquake in U.S. history happened in Alaska on March 27, 1964.

IN 1964, A DEADLY 9.2 MAGNITUDE EARTHQUAKE STRUCK IN ALASKA. IT CAUSED LANDSLIDES IN ALASKA AND TSUNAMIS AS FAR AWAY AS CALIFORNIA AND HAWAII.

UNDERWATER LANDSLIDES

An underwater landslide is called a submarine landslide. The force from one can greatly stir up the ocean above it. A submarine landslide might even cause a tsunami (soo-NAH-mee), or huge tidal wave. Tsunamis can wreck coastal villages. In 1998, a submarine landslide caused a tsunami that caused great harm in Papua New Guinea.

HURRICANES AND LANDSLIDES

Hurricanes bring strong winds and very heavy rains. Sometimes the earth in an area can't take all that extra water in, and neither can storm drain systems built by people. With nowhere else to go, the water just stays at the surface. This adds weight and reduces friction on steep, unstable slopes.

Hurricane Mitch struck Central America in October 1998. During this storm, rain fell at a rate of more than 4 inches (10.2 cm) per hour. This caused a huge lahar on the Casita volcano in Nicaragua. The debris traveled about 3.7 miles (6 km) down the slope of the volcano. About 2,500 people died In its course.

RAINFALL FROM HURRICANE MARIA, WHICH HIT PUERTO RICO IN 2017, CAUSED MORE THAN 40,000 SEPARATE LANDSLIDES AND MUDSLIDES AROUND THE ISLAND.

EYE OF THE STORM

Weather scientists call almost any rotating storm that forms over tropical water a tropical cyclone. In the Atlantic and northeast Pacific oceans, these are called hurricanes. In the northwest Pacific, they're called typhoons. Weaker cyclones are called tropical depressions or tropical storms. The rain from any of these can cause a landslide, especially in a mountainous area.

CAN WE PREVENT THEM?

Scientists can learn a lot by studying how and when past landslides reshaped Earth. That data can help them build models that **predict** where a landslide is likely to happen next. Scientists at NASA, the National Aeronautics and Space Administration, are using the internet to build the first-ever global database of landslides.

In 2018, NASA began asking regular people from all over the world to upload reports of landslides near them. These citizen scientists can log in and report the time, date, and location of the slide. The USGS also started a searchable online map of landslides in 2019.

NEW CRACKS IN A SIDEWALK COULD BE A SIGN THAT CONDITIONS ARE RIGHT FOR A LANDSLIDE. HOWEVER, THERE ARE MANY REASONS SIDEWALKS GET CRACKS. MOST OF THE TIME, IT DOESN'T MEAN A LANDSLIDE IS COMING.

WARNING SIGNS

Sometimes, Earth gives slight clues that conditions are right for a landslide. Roads or sidewalks could suddenly sink down or bulge up. Fences or telephone poles might lean at a funny angle. Strange sounds like rumbling, trees cracking, or rocks knocking together might mean that debris is falling nearby.

Not every landslide is big enough to make the news. That's why NASA needs reports about all landslides, even small ones. The database is just one of many ways to study landslides. Scientists can also study landslides from space!

NASA and other countries have sent **satellites** into space that take pictures of Earth. These satellites can tell them things such as how much rain an area gets, how steep a slope is, and where trees have disappeared. Scientists put these bits of data together to understand where a landslide might happen next. Satellites can also take pictures of landslide damage.

APRIL 20   MAY 17   MAY 22

HIGHWAY 1   HIGHWAY 1   HIGHWAY 1

IN 2017, A NASA SATELLITE TOOK PHOTOS BEFORE AND AFTER A MASSIVE MUDSLIDE SPILLED MORE THAN 1 MILLION TONS (0.9 MILLION MT) OF DEBRIS ALONG CALIFORNIA'S FAMOUS HIGHWAY 1.

OTHER METHODS TO STOP LANDSLIDES

Engineers, or scientists who plan and build things, use construction methods to prevent landslides. Retaining walls help keep the land behind them from sliding. You may have seen these giant walls near roads or buildings constructed near a slope. Planting trees can stop erosion and hold soil in place to prevent landslides too.

OUR CHANGING PLANET

Humans reshape Earth in major ways. We build roads and neighborhoods. We burn fossil fuels to power our cars. As the population grows, we construct giant factory farms to grow food. All of this contributes to climate change and global warming.

Climate change can change weather patterns that can cause landslides. Heavy rains and melting ice can trigger avalanches and mudslides. Human activity, such as mining and drilling for fossil fuels, can also make Earth's crust less stable. Remember, everything on Earth is connected. It's up to us to make changes to protect Earth for future generations.

RISING TEMPERATURES CAN THAW EARTH'S PERMAFROST, OR A DEEP LAYER OF SOIL THAT STAYS FROZEN FOR AT LEAST TWO YEARS. THIS MAKES MOUNTAINS LESS STABLE AND MORE PRONE TO LANDSLIDES.

A STORM IS BREWING

Rising temperatures in the air and water can cause severe weather such as hurricanes and tropical storms. While climate change doesn't cause more hurricanes to happen, it might be making them stronger. Research shows that global warming may lead to more severe hurricanes with higher wind speeds and heavier rain.

GLOSSARY

complex: having to do with something with many parts that work together

damage: harm. Also, to cause harm.

debris: the remains of something that has been broken

earthquake: a shaking of the ground caused by the movement of Earth's crust

erode: to wear away outer layers of rock or soil by the action of wind, water, or living things

factor: something that helps produce or influence a result

magnitude: a measure of the power of an earthquake

predict: to guess what will happen in the future based on facts or knowledge

refer: to have a direct connection or relationship to something

satellite: an object that circles Earth in order to collect and send information or aid in communication

transportation: the act of moving people or things from one place to another

trigger: to cause something to start or happen

volcano: an opening in a planet's surface through which hot, liquid rock sometimes flows

FOR MORE INFORMATION

BOOKS

Brundle, Joanna. *Landslides and Avalanches.* New York, NY: KidHaven Publishing, 2019.

Maurer, Daniel and Teresa Alberini. *Do You Really Want to Create a Mudslide? A Book About Erosion.* Mankato, MN: Amicus, 2017.

Meister, Cari. *Landslides.* Minneapolis, MN: Jump!, 2016.

WEBSITES

Landslide Hazards—An Awareness Guide
geologycafe.com/landslide/activities.html
Learn how to make your own landslide in this hands-on lab activity.

Landslides
www.weatherwizkids.com/?page_id=1326
See maps and satellite photos and read more surprising facts about landslides in U.S. history.

What Causes Mudslides?
www.wonderopolis.org/wonder/what-causes-mudslides
Get interesting facts about mudslides and find ideas for science projects here.

Publisher's note to educators and parents: Our editors have carefully reviewed these websites to ensure that they are suitable for students. Many websites change frequently, however, and we cannot guarantee that a site's future contents will continue to meet our high standards of quality and educational value. Be advised that students should be closely supervised whenever they access the internet.

INDEX

Alaska 20, 21

avalanche 7, 28

climate change 28, 29

countries 15, 26

creep 13

database 24, 26

falls 7, 10, 11, 16

flow 9, 10, 12, 13, 16

friction 20, 22

geology 8

gravity 6, 20

human activity 8, 28

hurricanes 22, 23, 29

lahar 7, 16, 22

mass wasting 5, 6

morphology 8

Mount Saint Helens 18, 19

mudflow 9, 12, 13

NASA 24, 26, 27

rain 6, 9, 14, 17, 19, 22, 23, 26, 28, 29

retaining walls 27

roads 5, 9, 16, 25, 27, 28

slides 10, 24

slope 6, 7, 9, 10, 12, 14, 22, 26, 27

speeds 4, 29

spread 10, 12, 16

topples 10

trees 4, 7, 13, 18, 25, 26, 27

tsunamis 21

USGS 15, 16, 24

Yosemite National Park 11